Please check all items for damages
before leaving the Library.
Thereafter you will be held
responsible for all injuries
to items beyond reasonable wear.

Helen M. Plum Memorial Library

Lombard, Illinois

A daily fine will be charged for
overdue materials.

AUG   2002

RESCUE BOATS

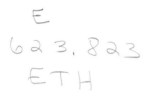

Please visit our web site at: www.garethstevens.com
For a free color catalog describing Gareth Stevens Publishing's
list of high-quality books and multimedia programs,
call 1-800-542-2595 or fax your request to (414) 332-3567.

Library of Congress Cataloging-in-Publication Data available upon request from publisher.
Fax (414) 336-0157 for the attention of the Publishing Records Department.

ISBN 0-8368-3048-2

First published in 2002 by
Gareth Stevens Publishing
A World Almanac Education Group Company
330 West Olive Street, Suite 100
Milwaukee, WI 53212 USA

Text and photos: Eric Ethan
Cover design and page layout: Tammy Gruenewald

This edition © 2002 by Gareth Stevens, Inc.

Printed in the United States of America

1 2 3 4 5 6 7 8 9 06 05 04 03 02

EMERGENCY VEHICLES

RESCUE BOATS

by Eric Ethan

Helen Plum Library
Lombard, IL

Gareth Stevens Publishing
A WORLD ALMANAC EDUCATION GROUP COMPANY

This is a rescue boat. Rescue boats find and help people who are in danger on the water.

Rescue boats have sirens and flashing lights to let people know they are coming to help. Can you find the siren and flashing light on this boat?

A big wheel steers the boat. Control levers near the wheel make the boat go faster or slower.

An engine gives the boat power. A special cover keeps the engine dry.

Sometimes a diver is needed to rescue someone in the water. Divers wear wet suits and flippers. An air tank helps them breathe underwater.

A wooden platform at the back of the boat makes getting in and out of the water easier.

There are different types of rescue boats. This boat has a flat bottom so it can go in shallow water where a bigger boat cannot go.

Every rescue boat has first aid equipment on it. This equipment is used to help people who are hurt.

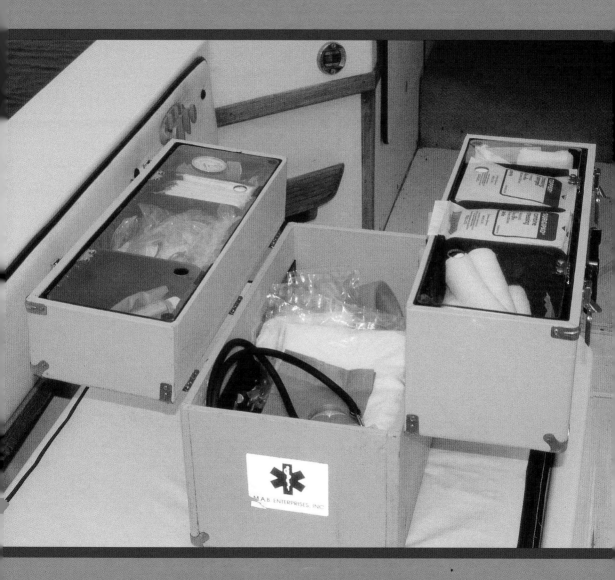

The crew on a rescue boat is trained to use the boat and its equipment. This crew is ready for duty!

GLOSSARY

control levers (kun-TROLL LEH-vers): metal rods that are moved to make a boat go faster or slower.

equipment (ee-KWIP-ment): the tools a person uses to do a job.

platform (PLAT-form): something a diver stands on to get into a boat.

sirens (SIE-ren): machines that make a loud warning noise.

wet suit (WET-soot): skin-tight clothing worn by a diver in cold water to keep the diver warm.

MORE BOOKS TO READ

Boats. Shana Corey (Random House)

Boats. On the Move (series).
Paul Stickland (Gareth Stevens)

Harbor. Donald Crews (Greenwillow Books)

WEB SITES

United States Coast Guard Kids Corner
www.uscg.mil/hq/g-cp/kids/kidindxx.html

Volunteer Marine Rescue Association
www.vmrsouthport.com

Water Rescue Craft
www.ses.vic.gov.au/boats.html

INDEX